QUEENS OF THE ANIMAL UNIVERSE

FEMALE SPOTTED HYENAS

Commanders of the Clan

by Jaclyn Jaycox

PEBBLE
a capstone imprint

Published by Pebble, an imprint of Capstone
1710 Roe Crest Drive
North Mankato, Minnesota 56003
capstonepub.com

Library of Congress Cataloging-in-Publication Data
Names: Jaycox, Jaclyn, 1983- author.
Title: Female spotted hyenas : commanders of the clan / by Jaclyn Jaycox.
Description: North Mankato, Minnesota : Pebble, [2023] | Series: Queens of the animal universe | Includes bibliographical references and index. | Audience: Ages 5-8 | Audience: Grades K-1 | Summary: "A group of spotted hyenas has just killed a gazelle. It's time to eat! But not every hyena digs in at once. The females eat first. Next, cubs eat, and then the males. In a hyena clan, females rule! They hunt, care for young, and protect the clan's territory. Take a look at spotted hyenas and the important roles females play to ensure the clan's survival"-- Provided by publisher.
Identifiers: LCCN 2021054294 (print) | LCCN 2021054295 (ebook) | ISBN 9781666343076 (hardcover) | ISBN 9781666343137 (paperback) | ISBN 9781666343199 (pdf) | ISBN 9781666343311 (kindle edition) Subjects: LCSH: Spotted hyena--Behavior--Juvenile literature. | Social hierarchy in animals--Juvenile literature. | Social behavior in animals--Juvenile literature. | Animal societies--Juvenile literature.
Classification: LCC QL737.C24 J39 2023 (print) | LCC QL737.C24 (ebook) | DDC 599.74/315--dc23/eng/20211122
LC record available at https://lccn.loc.gov/2021054294
LC ebook record available at https://lccn.loc.gov/2021054295

Editorial Credits
Editor: Carrie Sheely; Designer: Bobbie Nuytten; Media Researcher: Morgan Walters; Production Specialist: Polly Fisher

Image Credits
Alamy: AfriPics.com, 20, JEAN-FR@NCOIS DUCASSE, 5, Unlisted Images, Inc., 19; Capstone Press, 7; Shutterstock: Abdelrahman Hassanein, 26, 27, Amitrane, 9, Apostrophe_S, 28, BrightRainbow, (dots background) design element, Daniel-Alvarez, 15, francesco de marco, 29, Henk Bogaard, 23, Lazlow59, 17, Marion Feige-Muller, 25, matthieu Gallet, 10, NaturesMomentsuk, 6, PACO COMO, 21, Peter van Dam, 11, Sam DCruz, 14, Shams Ashraf, Cover, Trevor Fairbank, 13, WinWin artlab, (crowns) design element

Table of Contents

Females Rule!.................................... 4

Meet the Spotted Hyena 6

Hyena Bodies.................................10

Hyena Families 14

Ladies First.....................................16

Working Together............................ 22

Amazing Spotted Hyena Facts ...28

Glossary.................................30

Read More....................................31

Internet Sites.................................31

Index 32

Words in **bold** are in the glossary.

Females Rule!

In the animal world, males are often the leaders. They protect their families. They bring home the food. But this is not the case for spotted hyenas. The females are in charge! They are bigger and stronger than the males. These fearless females rule their family groups. Let's learn more about female spotted hyenas!

Female hyenas protect their families from any threats.

Meet the Spotted Hyena

Hyenas are a kind of **mammal**. Mammals have hair. Young mammals drink milk from their mothers.

There are four kinds of hyenas. Spotted hyenas are the biggest hyenas.

Hyenas often roam in the African savanna.

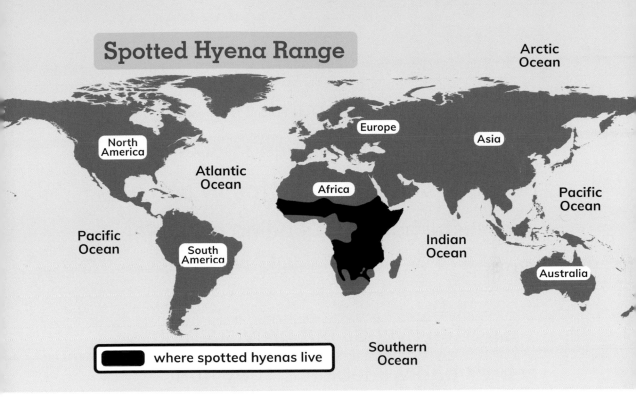

Spotted Hyena Range

Arctic Ocean

North America

Atlantic Ocean

Europe

Asia

Africa

Pacific Ocean

Pacific Ocean

South America

Indian Ocean

Australia

where spotted hyenas live

Southern Ocean

Spotted hyenas live in Africa. They are found in different kinds of **habitats**. They live in woodlands and flat, grassy areas called **savannas**. They also live in swampy areas and in mountain forests.

Loud whooping sounds ring out over the savanna. A hyena perks up her ears. She knows her family had a successful hunt. She's being called for dinner!

Spotted hyenas eat **prey** such as zebras and wildebeest. They hunt gazelles and warthogs too. They can even take down a young hippo! Hyenas sometimes are **scavengers**. They eat leftovers from another animal's meal. But they catch most of their own food.

Hyenas eat all parts of their prey. They even eat hooves, teeth, and bones! They throw up hair and hooves later. Their bodies can't break down these parts.

Hyenas get as much meat as they can from the body of a hippo.

Hyena Bodies

Spotted hyenas have red-brown, beige, tan, or yellow-gray coats. They are covered in dark spots. Each hyena's spots are different. Spotted hyenas also have short manes on their necks.

Spotted hyenas have rounded ears. This sets them apart from other types of hyenas that have pointy ears.

Spotted hyenas have strong senses of smell and hearing. They also have great vision, even in the dark. These senses help them hunt at night.

Hyenas are often active at night.

Spotted hyenas can weigh up to 190 pounds (86 kilograms). Males and females look alike. Their size helps people tell them apart. Females are a little bigger than males.

Spotted hyenas have powerful jaws. They have one of the strongest bites of all mammals. They can easily crush bones.

A hyena's jaws are lined with teeth that help them crush bones.

Hyena Families

Hyenas live in groups called clans. Clans can have more than 80 hyenas. Females stay in the same clan their whole lives. Males leave at around 3 years old. They join new clans.

Hyenas keep watch over their territory.

Hee-hee-hee! That's not a human laughing. It's a spotted hyena! These animals use different sounds to **communicate**. They are often called laughing hyenas for their well-known giggles. Some scientists think they laugh when they are frustrated. Spotted hyenas also grunt, squeal, and howl.

Spotted hyenas make more than 11 different sounds.

Ladies First

A male spotted hyena joins a new clan. But it is not a warm welcome. The females run the show. They will call him if he's needed. He may have to help scare off an animal that has come into the clan's **territory**. He may be chosen by a female to **mate**. But for now, he stays out of the way.

The male will hunt for food. But he has to eat fast! If he is caught by a female, he might lose his dinner. Females and their cubs always eat first.

Hyenas with the lowest ranks wait until those with higher ranks finish eating.

One female leads a clan. But all females rank higher than males. Even newborn cubs are above the males. New males to a clan rank lowest.

Many male animals fight over females. But not spotted hyenas. Females take the lead. They choose which males to mate with.

Female hyenas look out over their living area in Kenya, Africa.

Females give birth in dens. The dens are often underground. Lions attack hyena cubs. The dens help keep the cubs safe.

A hyena cub looks out of its den.

A mother usually gives birth to one to three cubs at a time. Newborn cubs have dark fur. They have teeth and their eyes are open.

The cubs depend on their mother. Her milk is their only food source for about six months.

A young hyena cub drinks milk from its mother.

Working Together

Ruling a hyena clan is no easy task! Females have many jobs.

Male hyenas don't help care for the young. Females raise cubs on their own. At two to six weeks, the mother moves the cubs to a larger den. Other mothers and cubs live there too.

The females help each other. When a mother has to hunt, other females stay with the cubs until their mother returns.

Two female hyenas stand
with cubs near their den.

In the larger den, the cubs meet one another. They learn their ranks. They play with other hyenas. This teaches them fighting skills. Higher-ranking cubs are more **aggressive** than lower-ranking ones.

Cubs stay in or near the den for the first year. Mothers teach their older cubs how to hunt. The young learn their territory. After about two years, cubs are ready to live without help.

Cubs begin to eat meat at about 5 months old.

Female spotted hyenas hunt a lot. Sometimes they hunt alone. They also hunt in small groups. But for large prey, they need a big group. They may call in males to help.

Large prey such as wildebeest can feed many hyenas.

Spotted hyenas protect their territory. Females are more willing to fight than males. They will even gather to chase off a lion!

Female spotted hyenas are key to a clan's survival. They hunt to feed the clan. They raise cubs and protect their families. They are amazing animal queens!

Hyenas chase off a lion.

Amazing Spotted Hyena Facts

A hyena's laugh can be heard by other hyenas 3 miles (5 kilometers) away!

Spotted hyenas are super smart! In tests, they did well solving problems using teamwork.

Spotted hyenas live a long time compared to other meat-eating mammals. They can live more than 20 years in the wild.

Spotted hyenas have large lungs and hearts. They can chase after prey for a long time before getting tired.

Lions and humans are the only two predators of spotted hyenas.

Spotted hyenas are not picky eaters. But they are big eaters! They can eat up to 35 pounds (16 kg) of meat in one meal.

Spotted hyenas use sounds to find each other when they are separated.

Hyenas look similar to dogs. But they are more closely related to cats.

Glossary

aggressive (uh-GREH-siv)—strong and forceful

communicate (kuh-MYOO-nuh-kate)—to share thoughts, feelings, or information

habitat (HAB-uh-tat)—the natural place and conditions in which an animal or plant lives

mammal (MAM-uhl)—a warm–blooded animal that breathes air; mammals have hair or fur; female mammals feed milk to their young

mate (MATE)—to join together to produce young

prey (PRAY)—an animal hunted by another animal for food

savanna (suh-VAN-uh)—a flat, grassy area of land with few or no trees

scavenger (SKAV-uhn-jer)—an animal that feeds on animals that are already dead

territory (TERR-uh-tor-ee)—the land on which an animal grazes or hunts for food and raises its young

Read More

Levy, Janey. *Hyenas Bite!* New York: Gareth Stevens Publishing, 2021.

Murray, Julie. *Spotted Hyena.* Edina, MN: Abdo Zoom, 2021.

Schuh, Mari. *Animals of the African Savanna.* North Mankato, MN: Capstone, 2022.

Internet Sites

Ducksters: Spotted Hyena
ducksters.com/animals/spotted_hyena.php

National Geographic Kids: Spotted Hyena Facts
natgeokids.com/uk/discover/animals/general-animals/spotted-hyena-facts/

San Diego Zoo Wildlife Alliance: Spotted Hyena
animals.sandiegozoo.org/animals/spotted-hyena

Index

bites, 12
bones, 9, 12, 13

clans, 14, 16, 18, 22, 27
coats, 10
cubs, 16, 18, 20, 21, 22, 23, 24, 25, 27

dens, 20, 22, 23, 24

giggles, 15

habitats, 7
hearing, 11
hunting, 8, 11, 16, 22, 24, 26, 27, 29

jaws, 12, 13

laughing, 15, 28

males, 4, 12, 14, 16, 18, 22, 26, 27
mammals, 6, 12, 28
manes, 10
mating, 16, 18

predators, 29
prey, 8, 9, 26, 29

ranks, 17, 18, 24

scavengers, 8
size, 4, 6, 12
smelling, 11
sounds, 8, 15, 28, 29

teeth, 9, 13, 21
territories, 14, 16, 24, 27

vision, 11

Author Biography

Behind the Lens Photography

Jaclyn Jaycox is a children's book author and editor. When she's not writing, she loves reading and spending time with her family. She lives in southern Minnesota with her husband, two kids, and a spunky goldendoodle.